Our Camping Trips

SUNSET SPLENDOR BOOKS

Included in this book:

Camping Supply List
Since everyone has their own specific needs and supplies, the lines are blank so that you can write out the items that you need to bring on your trips.
These two pages are in the front of the book, so your list will be easy to find and refer to for each trip.

Campground Review Pages
Four pages for each campground consisting of:
1. Specifics about the campground that you visited (name, date, address, reservation information, amenities, etc). Added to this page is also an area to comment on your specific campsite and note other campsites that you might consider staying at in the future.
2. A page to detail your experiences while you were there. This page includes activities you may have partaken in (hiking trails, water sports, games), and it gives you a spot to jot down areas of interest that are nearby.
3. A page to record food from this trip (whether you made it at the campsite or stopped at a local eatery), and a few lines to jot down new friends' names and contact information.
4. A lined page for anything else you may want to keep a record of from this camping trip.
   (There are pages to review up to twenty-four separate campgrounds.)

Rainy Day Resources
These are just a few pages with simple paper games that you can play while waiting for the sun to come out again.

Meal Planning Pages
These are pages where you can record what you are planning for breakfast, lunch, and dinner for each day of the week and a small shopping list area.
Many of us have our favorite camping meals so the meal planner could be used over and over again.

Camping Recipes
Each page in this section has room for two recipes to be written out. There are ten pages giving you the opportunity to write out twenty recipes.

Packing List!

_____   _____

_____   _____

_____   _____

_____   _____

_____   _____

_____   _____

_____   _____

_____   _____

_____   _____

_____   _____

_____   _____

_____   _____

_____   _____

_____   _____

_____   _____

_____   _____

_____   _____

_____   _____

_____   _____

Packing List!

_____   _____

_____   _____

_____   _____

_____   _____

_____   _____

_____   _____

_____   _____

_____   _____

_____   _____

_____   _____

_____   _____

_____   _____

_____   _____

_____   _____

_____   _____

_____   _____

_____   _____

_____   _____

Campground & Campsite Information

Date: _____

Campsite Name: _____

Address: _____

Reservation Information & Pricing: _____

_____

Campground Amenities:

Water:_____ Sewer:_____ Electric:_____ WiFi:_____

Laundry:_____ Security: _____ Store: _____

Bathrooms & Showers: _____

Pet Rules & Restrictions: _____

Water Features: _____

Any other comments about the campground: _____

_____

_____

Our Site:

Our Site Number: _____

Site Description: _____

_____

_____

Other sites to consider for future stays: _____

_____

Our Visit

Set Up & Tear Down Experience:_____

_____

_____

Weather: _____

_____

Activities:

Trails: _____

_____

Games: Volleyball, Tennis, Golf etc.

_____

_____

Water Sports: Fishing, Swimming, Boating, etc.

_____

_____

Nearby Attractions: Natural Wonders, Historic Sites, Theme Parks, Shopping, etc.

_____

_____

_____

_____

Our Camping Meals

Some of our favorite camping meals from this trip:

_____

_____

_____

_____

_____

_____

_____

_____

_____

_____

Friends that we made and their contact information:

_____

_____

_____

_____

_____

Everything Else

Campground & Campsite Information

Date: _____

Campsite Name: _____

Address: _____

Reservation Information & Pricing: _____

_____

Campground Amenities:

Water:_____ Sewer:_____ Electric:_____ WiFi:_____

Laundry:_____ Security: _____ Store: _____

Bathrooms & Showers: _____

Pet Rules & Restrictions: _____

Water Features: _____

Any other comments about the campground: _____

_____

_____

Our Site:

Our Site Number: _____

Site Description: _____

_____

_____

Other sites to consider for future stays: _____

_____

Our Visit

Set Up & Tear Down Experience:_____

_____

_____

Weather: _____

_____

Activities:

Trails: _____

_____

Games: Volleyball, Tennis, Golf etc.

_____

_____

Water Sports: Fishing, Swimming, Boating, etc.

_____

_____

Nearby Attractions: Natural Wonders, Historic Sites, Theme Parks, Shopping, etc.

_____

_____

_____

_____

Our Camping Meals

Some of our favorite camping meals from this trip:

_____

_____

_____

_____

_____

_____

_____

_____

_____

_____

Friends that we made and their contact information:

_____

_____

_____

_____

_____

Everything Else

Campground & Campsite Information

Date: _____

Campsite Name: _____

Address: _____

Reservation Information & Pricing: _____

_____

<u>Campground Amenities</u>:

Water:_____ Sewer:_____ Electric:_____ WiFi:_____

Laundry:_____ Security: _____ Store: _____

Bathrooms & Showers: _____

Pet Rules & Restrictions: _____

Water Features: _____

Any other comments about the campground: _____

_____

_____

<u>Our Site</u>:

Our Site Number: _____

Site Description: _____

_____

_____

Other sites to consider for future stays: _____

_____

Our Visit

Set Up & Tear Down Experience:_____

_____

_____

Weather: _____

_____

<u>Activities:</u>

Trails: _____

_____

Games: Volleyball, Tennis, Golf etc.

_____

_____

Water Sports: Fishing, Swimming, Boating, etc.

_____

_____

Nearby Attractions: Natural Wonders, Historic Sites, Theme Parks, Shopping, etc.

_____

_____

_____

_____

Our Camping Meals

Some of our favorite camping meals from this trip:

_____

_____

_____

_____

_____

_____

_____

_____

_____

_____

Friends that we made and their contact information:

_____

_____

_____

_____

Everything Else

Campground & Campsite Information

Date: _____

Campsite Name: _____

Address: _____

Reservation Information & Pricing: _____

_____

Campground Amenities:

Water:_____ Sewer:_____ Electric:_____ WiFi:_____

Laundry:_____ Security: _____ Store: _____

Bathrooms & Showers: _____

Pet Rules & Restrictions: _____

Water Features: _____

Any other comments about the campground: _____

_____

_____

Our Site:

Our Site Number: _____

Site Description: _____

_____

_____

Other sites to consider for future stays: _____

_____

Our Visit

Set Up & Tear Down Experience:_____

_____

_____

Weather: _____

_____

<u>Activities:</u>

Trails: _____

_____

Games: Volleyball, Tennis, Golf etc.

_____

_____

Water Sports: Fishing, Swimming, Boating, etc.

_____

_____

Nearby Attractions: Natural Wonders, Historic Sites, Theme Parks, Shopping, etc.

_____

_____

_____

_____

Our Camping Meals

Some of our favorite camping meals from this trip:

_____

_____

_____

_____

_____

_____

_____

_____

_____

_____

Friends that we made and their contact information:

_____

_____

_____

_____

_____

Everything Else

_____

_____

_____

_____

_____

_____

_____

_____

_____

_____

_____

_____

_____

_____

_____

_____

_____

_____

_____

_____

Campground & Campsite Information

Date: _____

Campsite Name: _____

Address: _____

Reservation Information & Pricing: _____

_____

Campground Amenities:

Water:_____ Sewer:_____ Electric:_____ WiFi:_____

Laundry:_____ Security: _____ Store: _____

Bathrooms & Showers: _____

Pet Rules & Restrictions: _____

Water Features: _____

Any other comments about the campground: _____

_____

_____

Our Site:

Our Site Number: _____

Site Description: _____

_____

_____

Other sites to consider for future stays: _____

_____

Our Visit

Set Up & Tear Down Experience:_____

_____

_____

Weather: _____

_____

<u>Activities:</u>

Trails: _____

_____

Games: Volleyball, Tennis, Golf etc.

_____

_____

Water Sports: Fishing, Swimming, Boating, etc.

_____

_____

Nearby Attractions: Natural Wonders, Historic Sites, Theme
Parks, Shopping, etc.

_____

_____

_____

_____

Our Camping Meals

Some of our favorite camping meals from this trip:

_____

_____

_____

_____

_____

_____

_____

_____

_____

_____

_____

Friends that we made and their contact information:

_____

_____

_____

_____

_____

Everything Else

Campground & Campsite Information

Date: _____

Campsite Name: _____

Address: _____

Reservation Information & Pricing: _____

_____

Campground Amenities:

Water:_____ Sewer:_____ Electric:_____ WiFi:_____

Laundry:_____ Security: _____ Store: _____

Bathrooms & Showers: _____

Pet Rules & Restrictions: _____

Water Features: _____

Any other comments about the campground: _____

_____

_____

Our Site:

Our Site Number: _____

Site Description: _____

_____

_____

Other sites to consider for future stays: _____

_____

Our Visit

Set Up & Tear Down Experience:_____

_____

_____

Weather: _____

_____

Activities:

Trails: _____

_____

Games: Volleyball, Tennis, Golf etc.

_____

_____

Water Sports: Fishing, Swimming, Boating, etc.

_____

_____

Nearby Attractions: Natural Wonders, Historic Sites, Theme Parks, Shopping, etc.

_____

_____

_____

_____

Our Camping Meals

Some of our favorite camping meals from this trip:

_____

_____

_____

_____

_____

_____

_____

_____

_____

_____

Friends that we made and their contact information:

_____

_____

_____

_____

_____

Everything Else

Campground & Campsite Information

Date: _____

Campsite Name: _____

Address: _____

Reservation Information & Pricing: _____

_____

Campground Amenities:

Water:_____ Sewer:_____ Electric:_____ WiFi:_____

Laundry:_____ Security: _____ Store: _____

Bathrooms & Showers: _____

Pet Rules & Restrictions: _____

Water Features: _____

Any other comments about the campground: _____

_____

_____

Our Site:

Our Site Number: _____

Site Description: _____

_____

_____

Other sites to consider for future stays: _____

_____

Our Visit

Set Up & Tear Down Experience:_____

_____

_____

Weather: _____

_____

Activities:

Trails: _____

_____

Games: Volleyball, Tennis, Golf etc.

_____

_____

Water Sports: Fishing, Swimming, Boating, etc.

_____

_____

Nearby Attractions: Natural Wonders, Historic Sites, Theme Parks, Shopping, etc.

_____

_____

_____

_____

Our Camping Meals

Some of our favorite camping meals from this trip:

_____

_____

_____

_____

_____

_____

_____

_____

_____

_____

Friends that we made and their contact information:

_____

_____

_____

_____

_____

Everything Else

Campground & Campsite Information

Date: _____

Campsite Name: _____

Address: _____

Reservation Information & Pricing: _____

_____

Campground Amenities:

Water:_____ Sewer:_____ Electric:_____ WiFi:_____

Laundry:_____ Security: _____ Store: _____

Bathrooms & Showers: _____

Pet Rules & Restrictions: _____

Water Features: _____

Any other comments about the campground: _____

_____

_____

Our Site:

Our Site Number: _____

Site Description: _____

_____

_____

Other sites to consider for future stays: _____

_____

Our Visit

Set Up & Tear Down Experience:_____

_____

_____

Weather: _____

_____

Activities:

Trails: _____

_____

Games: Volleyball, Tennis, Golf etc.

_____

_____

Water Sports: Fishing, Swimming, Boating, etc.

_____

_____

Nearby Attractions: Natural Wonders, Historic Sites, Theme Parks, Shopping, etc.

_____

_____

_____

_____

Our Camping Meals

Some of our favorite camping meals from this trip:

_____

_____

_____

_____

_____

_____

_____

_____

_____

_____

Friends that we made and their contact information:

_____

_____

_____

_____

_____

Everything Else

Campground & Campsite Information

Date: _____

Campsite Name: _____

Address: _____

Reservation Information & Pricing: _____

_____

<u>Campground Amenities:</u>

Water:_____ Sewer:_____ Electric:_____ WiFi:_____

Laundry:_____ Security: _____ Store: _____

Bathrooms & Showers: _____

Pet Rules & Restrictions: _____

Water Features: _____

Any other comments about the campground: _____

_____

_____

<u>Our Site:</u>

Our Site Number: _____

Site Description: _____

_____

_____

Other sites to consider for future stays: _____

_____

Our Visit

Set Up & Tear Down Experience:_____

_____

_____

Weather: _____

_____

Activities:

Trails: _____

_____

Games: Volleyball, Tennis, Golf etc.

_____

_____

Water Sports: Fishing, Swimming, Boating, etc.

_____

_____

Nearby Attractions: Natural Wonders, Historic Sites, Theme Parks, Shopping, etc.

_____

_____

_____

_____

Our Camping Meals

Some of our favorite camping meals from this trip:

_____

_____

_____

_____

_____

_____

_____

_____

_____

_____

Friends that we made and their contact information:

_____

_____

_____

_____

_____

Everything Else

Campground & Campsite Information

Date: _____

Campsite Name: _____

Address: _____

Reservation Information & Pricing: _____

_____

Campground Amenities:

Water:_____ Sewer:_____ Electric:_____ WiFi:_____

Laundry:_____ Security: _____ Store: _____

Bathrooms & Showers: _____

Pet Rules & Restrictions: _____

Water Features: _____

Any other comments about the campground: _____

_____

_____

Our Site:

Our Site Number: _____

Site Description: _____

_____

_____

Other sites to consider for future stays: _____

_____

Our Visit

Set Up & Tear Down Experience: _____

_____

_____

Weather: _____

_____

<u>Activities</u>:

Trails: _____

_____

Games: Volleyball, Tennis, Golf etc.

_____

_____

Water Sports: Fishing, Swimming, Boating, etc.

_____

_____

Nearby Attractions: Natural Wonders, Historic Sites, Theme Parks, Shopping, etc.

_____

_____

_____

_____

Our Camping Meals

Some of our favorite camping meals from this trip:

_____

_____

_____

_____

_____

_____

_____

_____

_____

_____

Friends that we made and their contact information:

_____

_____

_____

_____

_____

Everything Else

Campground & Campsite Information

Date: _____

Campsite Name: _____

Address: _____

Reservation Information & Pricing: _____

_____

Campground Amenities:

Water:_____ Sewer:_____ Electric:_____ WiFi:_____

Laundry:_____ Security: _____ Store: _____

Bathrooms & Showers: _____

Pet Rules & Restrictions: _____

Water Features: _____

Any other comments about the campground: _____

_____

_____

Our Site:

Our Site Number: _____

Site Description: _____

_____

_____

Other sites to consider for future stays: _____

_____

Our Visit

Set Up & Tear Down Experience:_____

_____

_____

Weather: _____

_____

<u>Activities</u>:

Trails: _____

_____

Games: Volleyball, Tennis, Golf etc.

_____

_____

Water Sports: Fishing, Swimming, Boating, etc.

_____

_____

Nearby Attractions: Natural Wonders, Historic Sites, Theme Parks, Shopping, etc.

_____

_____

_____

_____

Our Camping Meals

Some of our favorite camping meals from this trip:

_____

_____

_____

_____

_____

_____

_____

_____

_____

_____

_____

Friends that we made and their contact information:

_____

_____

_____

_____

_____

Everything Else

Campground & Campsite Information

Date: _____

Campsite Name: _____

Address: _____

Reservation Information & Pricing: _____

_____

Campground Amenities:

Water:_____ Sewer:_____ Electric:_____ WiFi:_____

Laundry:_____ Security: _____ Store: _____

Bathrooms & Showers: _____

Pet Rules & Restrictions: _____

Water Features: _____

Any other comments about the campground: _____

_____

_____

Our Site:

Our Site Number: _____

Site Description: _____

_____

_____

Other sites to consider for future stays: _____

_____

Our Visit

Set Up & Tear Down Experience:_____

_____

_____

Weather: _____

_____

Activities:

Trails: _____

_____

Games: Volleyball, Tennis, Golf etc.

_____

_____

Water Sports: Fishing, Swimming, Boating, etc.

_____

_____

Nearby Attractions: Natural Wonders, Historic Sites, Theme Parks, Shopping, etc.

_____

_____

_____

_____

Our Camping Meals

Some of our favorite camping meals from this trip:

_____

_____

_____

_____

_____

_____

_____

_____

_____

_____

_____

Friends that we made and their contact information:

_____

_____

_____

_____

_____

Everything Else

Campground & Campsite Information

Date: _____

Campsite Name: _____

Address: _____

Reservation Information & Pricing: _____

_____

Campground Amenities:

Water:_____ Sewer:_____ Electric:_____ WiFi:_____

Laundry:_____ Security: _____ Store: _____

Bathrooms & Showers: _____

Pet Rules & Restrictions: _____

Water Features: _____

Any other comments about the campground: _____

_____

_____

Our Site:

Our Site Number: _____

Site Description: _____

_____

_____

Other sites to consider for future stays: _____

_____

Our Visit

Set Up & Tear Down Experience:_____

_____

_____

Weather: _____

_____

Activities:

Trails: _____

_____

Games: Volleyball, Tennis, Golf etc.

_____

_____

Water Sports: Fishing, Swimming, Boating, etc.

_____

_____

Nearby Attractions: Natural Wonders, Historic Sites, Theme Parks, Shopping, etc.

_____

_____

_____

_____

Our Camping Meals

Some of our favorite camping meals from this trip:

_____

_____

_____

_____

_____

_____

_____

_____

_____

_____

Friends that we made and their contact information:

_____

_____

_____

_____

_____

Everything Else

Campground & Campsite Information

Date: _____

Campsite Name: _____

Address: _____

Reservation Information & Pricing: _____

_____

Campground Amenities:

Water:_____ Sewer:_____ Electric:_____ WiFi:_____

Laundry:_____ Security: _____ Store: _____

Bathrooms & Showers: _____

Pet Rules & Restrictions: _____

Water Features: _____

Any other comments about the campground: _____

_____

_____

Our Site:

Our Site Number: _____

Site Description: _____

_____

_____

Other sites to consider for future stays: _____

_____

Our Visit

Set Up & Tear Down Experience:_____

_____

_____

Weather: _____

_____

Activities:

Trails: _____

_____

Games: Volleyball, Tennis, Golf etc.

_____

_____

Water Sports: Fishing, Swimming, Boating, etc.

_____

_____

Nearby Attractions: Natural Wonders, Historic Sites, Theme Parks, Shopping, etc.

_____

_____

_____

_____

Our Camping Meals

Some of our favorite camping meals from this trip:

_____

_____

_____

_____

_____

_____

_____

_____

_____

_____

Friends that we made and their contact information:

_____

_____

_____

_____

_____

Everything Else

Campground & Campsite Information

Date: _____

Campsite Name: _____

Address: _____

Reservation Information & Pricing: _____

_____

Campground Amenities:

Water:_____ Sewer:_____ Electric:_____ WiFi:_____

Laundry:_____ Security: _____ Store: _____

Bathrooms & Showers: _____

Pet Rules & Restrictions: _____

Water Features: _____

Any other comments about the campground: _____

_____

_____

Our Site:

Our Site Number: _____

Site Description: _____

_____

_____

Other sites to consider for future stays: _____

_____

Our Visit

Set Up & Tear Down Experience:_____

_____

_____

Weather: _____

_____

Activities:

Trails: _____

_____

Games: Volleyball, Tennis, Golf etc.

_____

_____

Water Sports: Fishing, Swimming, Boating, etc.

_____

_____

Nearby Attractions: Natural Wonders, Historic Sites, Theme
Parks, Shopping, etc.

_____

_____

_____

_____

Our Camping Meals

Some of our favorite camping meals from this trip:

_____

_____

_____

_____

_____

_____

_____

_____

_____

_____

Friends that we made and their contact information:

_____

_____

_____

_____

_____

Everything Else

Campground & Campsite Information

Date: _____

Campsite Name: _____

Address: _____

Reservation Information & Pricing: _____

_____

Campground Amenities:

Water:_____ Sewer:_____ Electric:_____ WiFi:_____

Laundry:_____ Security: _____ Store: _____

Bathrooms & Showers: _____

Pet Rules & Restrictions: _____

Water Features: _____

Any other comments about the campground: _____

_____

_____

Our Site:

Our Site Number: _____

Site Description: _____

_____

_____

Other sites to consider for future stays: _____

_____

Our Visit

Set Up & Tear Down Experience:_____

_____

_____

Weather: _____

_____

<u>Activities:</u>

Trails: _____

_____

Games: Volleyball, Tennis, Golf etc.

_____

_____

Water Sports: Fishing, Swimming, Boating, etc.

_____

_____

Nearby Attractions: Natural Wonders, Historic Sites, Theme
Parks, Shopping, etc.

_____

_____

_____

_____

Our Camping Meals

Some of our favorite camping meals from this trip:

_____

_____

_____

_____

_____

_____

_____

_____

_____

_____

Friends that we made and their contact information:

_____

_____

_____

_____

_____

Everything Else

Campground & Campsite Information

Date: _____

Campsite Name: _____

Address: _____

Reservation Information & Pricing: _____

_____

Campground Amenities:

Water:_____ Sewer:_____ Electric:_____ WiFi:_____

Laundry:_____ Security: _____ Store: _____

Bathrooms & Showers: _____

Pet Rules & Restrictions: _____

Water Features: _____

Any other comments about the campground: _____

_____

_____

Our Site:

Our Site Number: _____

Site Description: _____

_____

_____

Other sites to consider for future stays: _____

_____

Our Visit

Set Up & Tear Down Experience:_____

_____

_____

Weather: _____

_____

<u>Activities</u>:

Trails: _____

_____

Games: Volleyball, Tennis, Golf etc.

_____

_____

Water Sports: Fishing, Swimming, Boating, etc.

_____

_____

Nearby Attractions: Natural Wonders, Historic Sites, Theme Parks, Shopping, etc.

_____

_____

_____

_____

Our Camping Meals

Some of our favorite camping meals from this trip:

_____

_____

_____

_____

_____

_____

_____

_____

_____

_____

_____

Friends that we made and their contact information:

_____

_____

_____

_____

_____

Everything Else

Campground & Campsite Information

Date: _____

Campsite Name: _____

Address: _____

Reservation Information & Pricing: _____

_____

Campground Amenities:

Water:_____ Sewer:_____ Electric:_____ WiFi:_____

Laundry:_____ Security: _____ Store: _____

Bathrooms & Showers: _____

Pet Rules & Restrictions: _____

Water Features: _____

Any other comments about the campground: _____

_____

_____

Our Site:

Our Site Number: _____

Site Description: _____

_____

_____

Other sites to consider for future stays: _____

_____

Our Visit

Set Up & Tear Down Experience:_____

_____

_____

Weather: _____

_____

Activities:

Trails: _____

_____

Games: Volleyball, Tennis, Golf etc.

_____

_____

Water Sports: Fishing, Swimming, Boating, etc.

_____

_____

Nearby Attractions: Natural Wonders, Historic Sites, Theme Parks, Shopping, etc.

_____

_____

_____

_____

Our Camping Meals

Some of our favorite camping meals from this trip:

_____

_____

_____

_____

_____

_____

_____

_____

_____

_____

Friends that we made and their contact information:

_____

_____

_____

_____

_____

Everything Else

Campground & Campsite Information

Date: _____

Campsite Name: _____

Address: _____

Reservation Information & Pricing: _____

_____

Campground Amenities:

Water:_____ Sewer:_____ Electric:_____ WiFi:_____

Laundry:_____ Security: _____ Store: _____

Bathrooms & Showers: _____

Pet Rules & Restrictions: _____

Water Features: _____

Any other comments about the campground: _____

_____

_____

Our Site:

Our Site Number: _____

Site Description: _____

_____

_____

Other sites to consider for future stays: _____

_____

Our Visit

Set Up & Tear Down Experience:_____

_____

_____

Weather: _____

_____

Activities:

Trails: _____

_____

Games: Volleyball, Tennis, Golf etc.

_____

_____

Water Sports: Fishing, Swimming, Boating, etc.

_____

_____

Nearby Attractions: Natural Wonders, Historic Sites, Theme Parks, Shopping, etc.

_____

_____

_____

_____

Our Camping Meals

Some of our favorite camping meals from this trip:

_____

_____

_____

_____

_____

_____

_____

_____

_____

_____

Friends that we made and their contact information:

_____

_____

_____

_____

_____

Everything Else

Campground & Campsite Information

Date: _____

Campsite Name: _____

Address: _____

Reservation Information & Pricing: _____

_____

Campground Amenities:

Water:_____ Sewer:_____ Electric:_____ WiFi:_____

Laundry:_____ Security: _____ Store: _____

Bathrooms & Showers: _____

Pet Rules & Restrictions: _____

Water Features: _____

Any other comments about the campground: _____

_____

_____

Our Site:

Our Site Number: _____

Site Description: _____

_____

_____

Other sites to consider for future stays: _____

_____

Our Visit

Set Up & Tear Down Experience:_____

_____

_____

Weather: _____

_____

Activities:

Trails: _____

_____

Games: Volleyball, Tennis, Golf etc.

_____

_____

Water Sports: Fishing, Swimming, Boating, etc.

_____

_____

Nearby Attractions: Natural Wonders, Historic Sites, Theme Parks, Shopping, etc.

_____

_____

_____

_____

Our Camping Meals

Some of our favorite camping meals from this trip:

_____

_____

_____

_____

_____

_____

_____

_____

_____

_____

Friends that we made and their contact information:

_____

_____

_____

_____

_____

Everything Else

Campground & Campsite Information

Date: _____

Campsite Name: _____

Address: _____

Reservation Information & Pricing: _____

_____

<u>Campground Amenities</u>:

Water:_____ Sewer:_____ Electric:_____ WiFi:_____

Laundry:_____ Security: _____ Store: _____

Bathrooms & Showers: _____

Pet Rules & Restrictions: _____

Water Features: _____

Any other comments about the campground: _____

_____

_____

<u>Our Site</u>:

Our Site Number: _____

Site Description: _____

_____

_____

Other sites to consider for future stays: _____

_____

Our Visit

Set Up & Tear Down Experience:_____

_____

_____

Weather: _____

_____

<u>Activities:</u>

Trails: _____

_____

Games: Volleyball, Tennis, Golf etc.

_____

_____

Water Sports: Fishing, Swimming, Boating, etc.

_____

_____

Nearby Attractions: Natural Wonders, Historic Sites, Theme Parks, Shopping, etc.

_____

_____

_____

_____

Our Camping Meals

Some of our favorite camping meals from this trip:

_____

_____

_____

_____

_____

_____

_____

_____

_____

_____

_____

Friends that we made and their contact information:

_____

_____

_____

_____

_____

Everything Else

Campground & Campsite Information

Date: _____

Campsite Name: _____

Address: _____

Reservation Information & Pricing: _____

_____

Campground Amenities:

Water:_____ Sewer:_____ Electric:_____ WiFi:_____

Laundry:_____ Security: _____ Store: _____

Bathrooms & Showers: _____

Pet Rules & Restrictions: _____

Water Features: _____

Any other comments about the campground: _____

_____

_____

Our Site:

Our Site Number: _____

Site Description: _____

_____

_____

Other sites to consider for future stays: _____

_____

Our Visit

Set Up & Tear Down Experience:_____

_____

_____

Weather: _____

_____

<u>Activities:</u>

Trails: _____

_____

Games: Volleyball, Tennis, Golf etc.

_____

_____

Water Sports: Fishing, Swimming, Boating, etc.

_____

_____

Nearby Attractions: Natural Wonders, Historic Sites, Theme Parks, Shopping, etc.

_____

_____

_____

_____

Our Camping Meals

Some of our favorite camping meals from this trip:

_____

_____

_____

_____

_____

_____

_____

_____

_____

_____

Friends that we made and their contact information:

_____

_____

_____

_____

_____

Everything Else

Campground & Campsite Information

Date: _____

Campsite Name: _____

Address: _____

Reservation Information & Pricing: _____

_____

Campground Amenities:

Water:_____ Sewer:_____ Electric:_____ WiFi:_____

Laundry:_____ Security: _____ Store: _____

Bathrooms & Showers: _____

Pet Rules & Restrictions: _____

Water Features: _____

Any other comments about the campground: _____

_____

_____

Our Site:

Our Site Number: _____

Site Description: _____

_____

_____

Other sites to consider for future stays: _____

_____

Our Visit

Set Up & Tear Down Experience:_____

_____

_____

Weather: _____

_____

Activities:

Trails: _____

_____

Games: Volleyball, Tennis, Golf etc.

_____

_____

Water Sports: Fishing, Swimming, Boating, etc.

_____

_____

Nearby Attractions: Natural Wonders, Historic Sites, Theme Parks, Shopping, etc.

_____

_____

_____

_____

Our Camping Meals

Some of our favorite camping meals from this trip:

_____

_____

_____

_____

_____

_____

_____

_____

_____

_____

_____

Friends that we made and their contact information:

_____

_____

_____

_____

_____

Everything Else

Campground & Campsite Information

Date: _____

Campsite Name: _____

Address: _____

Reservation Information & Pricing: _____

_____

Campground Amenities:

Water:_____ Sewer:_____ Electric:_____ WiFi:_____

Laundry:_____ Security: _____ Store: _____

Bathrooms & Showers: _____

Pet Rules & Restrictions: _____

Water Features: _____

Any other comments about the campground: _____

_____

_____

Our Site:

Our Site Number: _____

Site Description: _____

_____

_____

Other sites to consider for future stays: _____

_____

Our Visit

Set Up & Tear Down Experience:_____

_____

_____

Weather: _____

_____

Activities:

Trails: _____

_____

Games: Volleyball, Tennis, Golf etc.

_____

_____

Water Sports: Fishing, Swimming, Boating, etc.

_____

_____

Nearby Attractions: Natural Wonders, Historic Sites, Theme Parks, Shopping, etc.

_____

_____

_____

_____

Our Camping Meals

Some of our favorite camping meals from this trip:

_____

_____

_____

_____

_____

_____

_____

_____

_____

_____

_____

Friends that we made and their contact information:

_____

_____

_____

_____

_____

Everything Else

Rainy Day Resources

On those rainy days when you may not have anything else to do, you may want to play some games to pass the time. Here are some simple game sheets that you can use.

Don't feed the animals!

Dots & Boxes

Instructions:
This is a game for two players.
Players take turns to connect two vertically or horizontally adjacent dots with a pencil.
Diagonal lines cannot be made.
The object is to draw a line to complete a square. When that is done, the player who completed the square puts his initial in the square that he has completed. He continues his turn until he cannot complete a square.
When all possible squares are created, the initials are counted and the one with the most boxes wins!

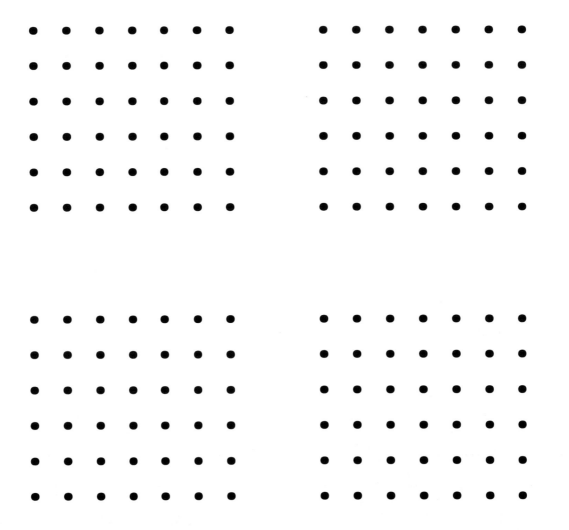

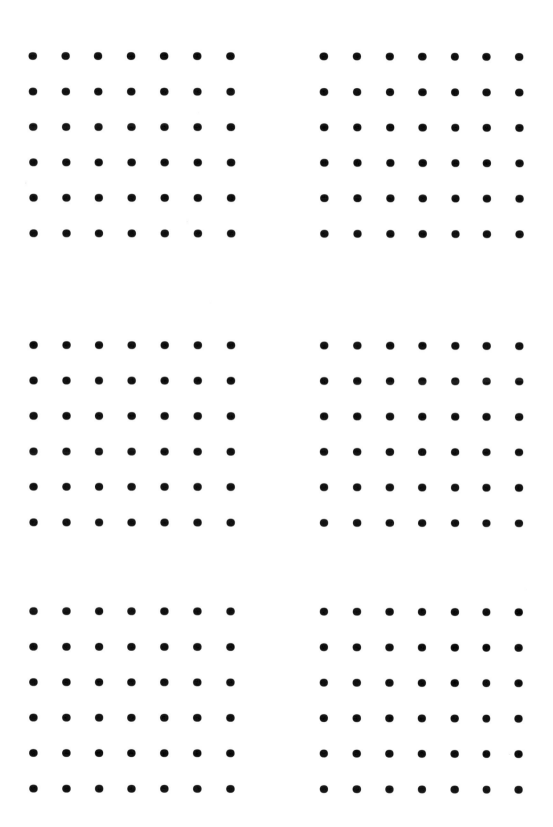

Four in a Row

Four in a Row is a simple turn-taking game that can be played two ways.

Instructions for version one--no gravity variation

This is a game for two players. They share a board.
Each player has a different color pen.
Players take turns to color any circle in their color.
The winner is the first person to connect four circles horizontally, vertically or diagonally.

Instructions for version two--gravity variation

Play the same as the above method, but players may only color the bottom-most empty circle in any column.

The winner is the first person to connect four circles horizontally, vertically or diagonally.

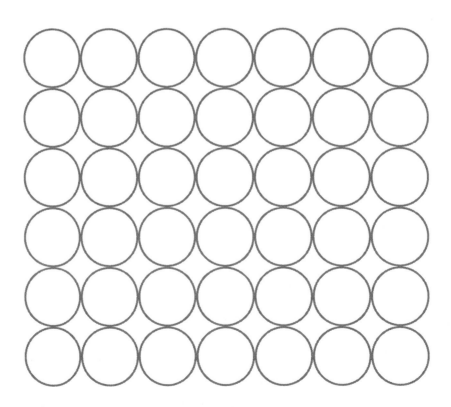

Tic Tac Toe

Instructions:
This is a game for two players.
One player chooses X and the other player chooses O
Each player takes turns placing their mark on the grid
The winner is the first player to get three in a row horizontally, vertically, or diagonally.
The game is tied if the board is filled without either player scoring a full row of three.

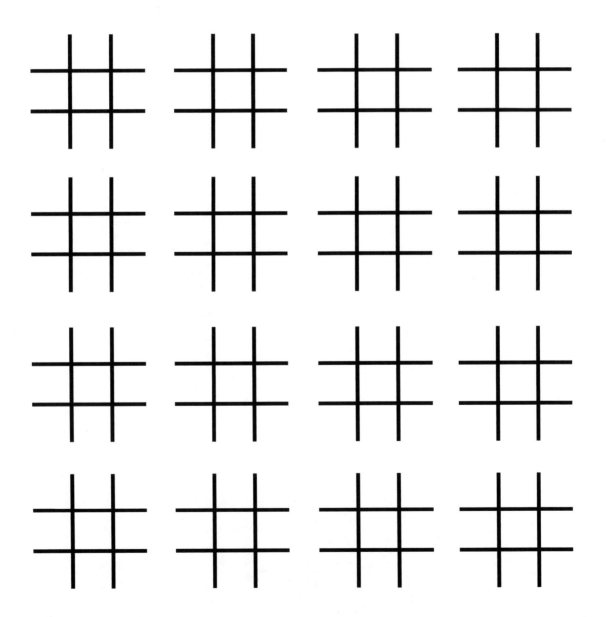

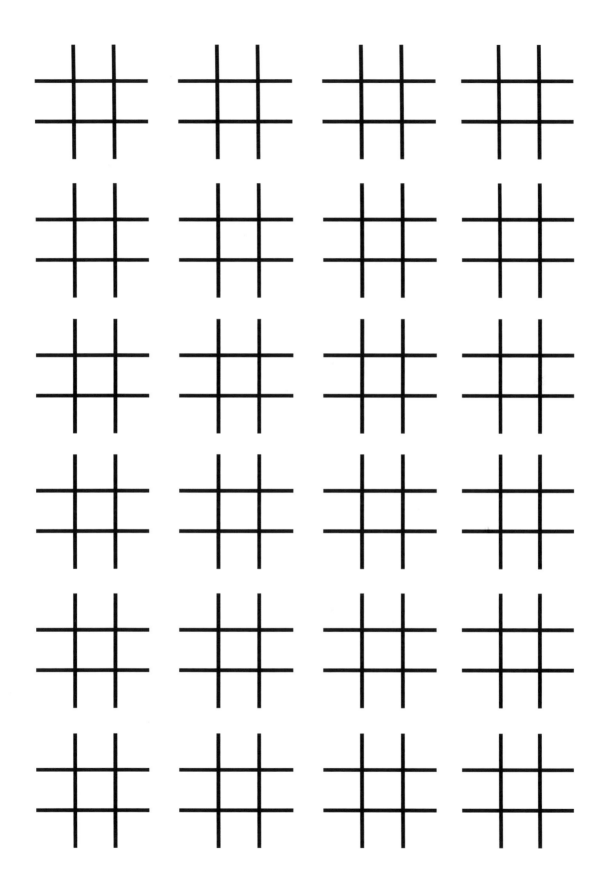

Make a Word

Instructions:
This is a game that can be played alone or with any number of players.
The object is to see how many words can be made using the letters in the below phrases. The one who makes the most words (or the most unusual word) in one minute (or any set amount of time) wins!

CAMPING IN THE GREAT OUTDOORS

_____	_____	_____
_____	_____	_____
_____	_____	_____
_____	_____	_____
_____	_____	_____
_____	_____	_____
_____	_____	_____
_____	_____	_____
_____	_____	_____
_____	_____	_____
_____	_____	_____
_____	_____	_____

Unscramble the Words

Instructions:
This is a game that can be played alone or with any number of players.
The object is to see how many scrambled words can be unscrambled in one minute
(or any set amount of time). [Solution on last page of book.]

1. AMESPRC   _____

2. ORMHUMOS   _____

3. ESRILRQU   _____

4. UIOSQMTO   _____

5. GNWMSMII   _____

6. HGKINI   _____

7. NUKKS   _____

8. CACONOR   _____

9. RILTA   _____

10. OSIOPIN VIY _____ _____

11. NSCORA   _____

12. EMKSO   _____

BONUS: WRALAMOSHLM

_____

Monday

B
L
D

Tuesday

B
L
D

Wednesday

B
L
D

Thursday

B
L
D

Friday

B
L
D

Saturday

B
L
D

Sunday

B
L
D

Date

Grocery List

Fruits & Veggies	Dairy
Meat	Frozen
Ingredients	Snacks

Snacks

Monday

B _____
L _____
D _____

Tuesday

B _____
L _____
D _____

Wednesday

B _____
L _____
D _____

Thursday

B _____
L _____
D _____

Friday

B _____
L _____
D _____

Saturday

B _____
L _____
D _____

Sunday

B _____
L _____
D _____

Date _____

Grocery List

Fruits & Veggies	Dairy
Meat	Frozen
Ingredients	Snacks

Snacks

_____
_____
_____
_____
_____
_____
_____

Monday

B _____
L _____
D _____

Tuesday

B _____
L _____
D _____

Wednesday

B _____
L _____
D _____

Thursday

B _____
L _____
D _____

Friday

B _____
L _____
D _____

Saturday

B _____
L _____
D _____

Sunday

B _____
L _____
D _____

Date _____

Grocery List

Fruits & Veggies	Dairy
Meat	Frozen
Ingredients	Snacks

Snacks

_____
_____
_____
_____
_____
_____
_____

Camping Recipes

Title: _____

Ingredients:

_____   _____
_____   _____
_____   _____
_____   _____

Instructions:

_____
_____
_____
_____
_____
_____

Title: _____

Ingredients:

_____   _____
_____   _____
_____   _____
_____   _____

Instructions:

_____
_____
_____
_____
_____
_____

Title: _____

Ingredients:

_____   _____
_____   _____
_____   _____
_____   _____

Instructions:

_____
_____
_____
_____
_____
_____
_____

Title: _____

Ingredients:

_____   _____
_____   _____
_____   _____
_____   _____

Instructions:

_____
_____
_____
_____
_____
_____
_____

Title: _____

Ingredients:

_____   _____
_____   _____
_____   _____
_____   _____

Instructions:

_____
_____
_____
_____
_____
_____

Title: _____

Ingredients:

_____   _____
_____   _____
_____   _____
_____   _____

Instructions:

_____
_____
_____
_____
_____
_____

Title: _____

Ingredients:

_____   _____
_____   _____
_____   _____
_____   _____

Instructions:

_____
_____
_____
_____
_____
_____
_____

Title: _____

Ingredients:

_____   _____
_____   _____
_____   _____
_____   _____

Instructions:

_____
_____
_____
_____
_____
_____
_____

Title: _____

Ingredients:

_____ _____
_____ _____
_____ _____
_____ _____

Instructions:

_____
_____
_____
_____
_____
_____
_____

Title: _____

Ingredients:

_____ _____
_____ _____
_____ _____
_____ _____

Instructions:

_____
_____
_____
_____
_____
_____
_____

Title: _____

Ingredients:

_____   _____
_____   _____
_____   _____
_____   _____

Instructions:

_____
_____
_____
_____
_____
_____
_____

Title: _____

Ingredients:

_____   _____
_____   _____
_____   _____
_____   _____

Instructions:

_____
_____
_____
_____
_____
_____
_____

Title: _____

Ingredients:

_____   _____
_____   _____
_____   _____
_____   _____

Instructions:

_____
_____
_____
_____
_____
_____
_____

Title: _____

Ingredients:

_____   _____
_____   _____
_____   _____
_____   _____

Instructions:

_____
_____
_____
_____
_____
_____
_____

Title: _____

Ingredients:

_____   _____
_____   _____
_____   _____
_____   _____

Instructions:

_____
_____
_____
_____
_____
_____
_____

Title: _____

Ingredients:

_____   _____
_____   _____
_____   _____
_____   _____

Instructions:

_____
_____
_____
_____
_____
_____
_____

Title: _____

Ingredients:

_____   _____
_____   _____
_____   _____
_____   _____

Instructions:

_____
_____
_____
_____
_____
_____

Title: _____

Ingredients:

_____   _____
_____   _____
_____   _____
_____   _____

Instructions:

_____
_____
_____
_____
_____
_____

Title: _____

Ingredients:

_____ _____
_____ _____
_____ _____
_____ _____

Instructions:

_____
_____
_____
_____
_____
_____
_____

Title: _____

Ingredients:

_____ _____
_____ _____
_____ _____
_____ _____

Instructions:

_____
_____
_____
_____
_____
_____

I hope you have enjoyed using this book and that you will continue to make many more memories.

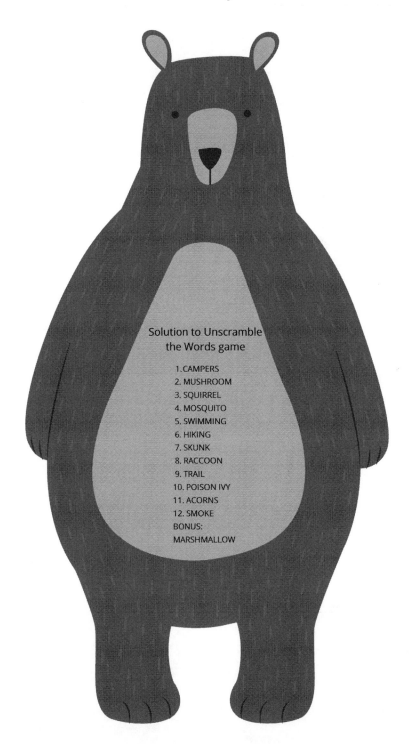

Solution to Unscramble
the Words game

1. CAMPERS
2. MUSHROOM
3. SQUIRREL
4. MOSQUITO
5. SWIMMING
6. HIKING
7. SKUNK
8. RACCOON
9. TRAIL
10. POISON IVY
11. ACORNS
12. SMOKE
BONUS:
MARSHMALLOW

Made in the USA
Columbia, SC
30 June 2025

60130388R00070